First published in Great Britain
in 2000 by Poetry Now
Remus House,
Coltsfoot Drive,
Woodston,
Peterborough, PE2 9JX
Telephone (01733) 898101
Fax (01733) 313524

HB ISBN 0 75430 835 9
SB ISBN 0 75430 836 7

Foreword

Poetry Now have successfully been producing
poetry for over 10 years, and as it is the poets' duty
to reach out and embrace the world with their
words, what better time to do this than when they
are young and eager to learn.

Over The Rainbow is for children of all ages. The
contents are varied and imaginative which will
enable your child to explore the world in which
they live. Every child should have the chance to
learn about poetry, especially in a fun and
enjoyable way.

Becki Mee, Editor

Contents

Monsters In The Dark

Stephen Hill

Are you afraid of the dark?
Lying in bed at night, covers pulled up to your chin
Listening to the monsters outside your window
Hoping they won't come in.

What about the creature under your bed?
Lying in wait for you
Make sure your arms and legs don't dangle
So he can't drag you under too.

A dark shape in the corner
That used to be clothes on the chair.
A hunchback ghoul watches you
Giving you an evil stare.

Noises up in the loft
It's a madman creeping about
What if he comes down from the attic?
You'll be too scared to shout.

Alone in bed can be scary at night
When you are just a child
But there's no reason to be afraid of the dark
It's only your imagination running wild.

Growing

Chris Stokes

I'm lying on the ground
With others just the same.
But then I'm carried in the air
Like I'm on a giant crane.
Oh no, I'm falling to the earth
I'll hit it with a thud
But no, I miss the rocks and stones
And plop into the mud.
It's dark in here but I can feel
That now I'm growing bigger.
And as the months go quickly by
I'm growing with some vigour.
For now I've changed,
Just look at me.
I'm not a seed . . .
I'm now a tree!

Open Your Mind

Samantha Tritton (10)

Open your mind and look inside,
Grab your imagination and stretch it wide.
There you will find a mystical land,
Full of hopes, dreams and a beach with golden sand.
You sleep in, in the morning with breakfast in bed,
A time to relax and rest your head.
Where fairies greet you and see to your every need,
As long as every day you do a good deed.
At the end of the week they give you praise,
For all of your hard work done in the previous days.
You will bounce on clouds and dance on stars,
Ice skate on Saturn's rings and visit Mars.
Sunbathe on the Sun and cool down on the Moon,
Talk to Venus when you're full of gloom.
Your best friend is an angel and her name is Buttercup,
She offers you a sacred drink in a golden cup.
Which gives you the power to gracefully fly,
To hope and dream and never to die.
To go to a beach where the Sun shines every day,
But only I can reach my mind because my mind
Is precious in every way.

Mummy Wouldn't Lie

Sally Slapcabbage

Mummy tells me that it's night,
But outside it's still light, Mummy wouldn't lie,
I believe her and go to bed,
Trying to remember things she said.
Like 'It will be tomorrow in the morning,'
As into a dream I am falling.
Outside I hear children playing,
'Be quiet' I hear Mummy saying. Mummy wouldn't lie.
When I wake I say 'Is it tomorrow now?'
She says 'No, it's today.' How?
She makes me go to bed when I'm wide awake,
I'm fast asleep in the morning, she gives me a shake.
'Eat your carrots, in the dark you will see.'
Doesn't make much sense to me.
Tooth fairy, Santa Claus,
I believe just because, Mummy wouldn't lie.
Dad says 'Don't forget the post or we'll get a fine,
Oh it's raining, she said the sun would shine.'
'Mummy my feet are wet, I need new shoes,
Can I have some, can I choose?'
I start to cry, my feet are wetter,
We walk past the post office, don't post the letter.
Mummy opens the letter and buys my new shoes,
Red, shiny ones with a buckle, I did choose.
If you want curly hair you must eat burnt toast,
Inspector calls for TV licence, she says 'It's in the post.'
Mummy wouldn't lie.
She says I'm the only one, I hear a baby cry,
I have to give *it* all my toys! Did Mummy tell a lie?

Animal Offerings

Heather Scully

Creamy-white coat and coal-black noses,
Furry all over from tips to toes-es!
Want your Polar Bear to linger? -
Give him ice-cold tea and a fishy-finger!

But . . .

If you give a bun to an Elephant,
He'll trumpet a big, loud - 'Thank-ie!'
But stay well clear if you give him a cold -
'Cos he blows on a huge great hankie!

Animal Salad

David Watts

I've seen lions in the jungle
standing over ten feet tall;
Giraffes creeping through the long grass,
three foot - neck 'n' all;
Tigers in the bush that hiss;
A snake who gave a roar;
But I've never seen a rabbit chase
an elephant before.

I've spotted hippopotami,
swinging tree to tree;
And monkeys basking in a lake,
while alligators flee;
A cheetah hiding in its shell,
As turtles make a kill;
But Oh to watch a bunny chase
A jumbo up a hill.

I've witnessed polar bears asleep,
on Massai Mara's plains,
as porcupines die laughing at
hyenas chasing cranes;
A herd of vultures grazing near,
while zebras hover high;
But not one elephant for dust,
as Brer goes hopping by.

I've even seen an ostrich as
it chased an angry bear;
Jumping rhinos; graceful wart hogs
leaping through the air;
A charging kangaroo - head down -
to me is nothing new;
So why won't Fluffy Bun stampede
an elephant or two?

Now if you have ambitions and,
they can't get off the ground,
try tossing facts up as they are,
and watch them fall around;
It's fun to see things taking shape -
although I must concede,
I've yet to see that rabbit run,
with Jumbo in the lead.

Our Child

Frances Dinsdale

Sleep our little one, have no cares
Let only sweet dreams be yours to share
Angels watch over you night and day
No harm will ever come your way
May tears in your life be few
We will always look after you
To see your child sleep peacefully
Is a mam and dad's delight
To know its love is freely given
Makes everything alright
And when the child awakes at dawn
And shouts for us at early morn
We'll be thankful for that new day
For in our lives you are here to stay.

Time

G McAviney

Why is it when you're having fun
Time goes by all too quickly?
The hands upon the mantle clock
Move Oh so swiftly.

But when one is, say, at school
And maths is on the menu,
Then time can be so cruel
It seems to know the venue.

I've even tried a little 'tool'
A matter of disguise
Yet time you just can't fool
No matter where you hide!

This proves that time is precious
Never knowing what is left
Enjoy each moment every day
No tears then may be wept.

Little Angel

Jacqui Bridgen

Little angel rest your head,
It's time for you to go to bed,
The smiling sun has said 'Goodbye,'
The moon is shining in the sky,
With little stars that twinkle so,
Sparkling in a magic glow.

Little angel close your eyes,
As I sing you sweet lullabies,
Let your dreams take you away,
To a magic place, where fairies play.
A place where nothing is as it seems,
The special magic land of dreams.

Little angel in gentle sleep,
Locked within your thoughts so deep,
Safe and warm within your bed,
I'll kiss you softly on your head,
It's time for me to say 'Goodnight.'
I'll see you in the morning light.

Amy's Friend

W G Lucas

amy's friend was born in a drain,
he swims up to hillsborough via belgium and spain.
his body is covered in blue monster hair,
he wears a sombrero and pink underwear.

amy's friend lives in a hole in the floor,
where he'll raise an umbrella when the rain starts to pour.
he doesn't mind dogs but despises the cats,
and will let them be blamed when he pees on the mats.

amy's friend may be small and uncouth
with his ragged appearance and his big pointy tooth.
but he looks after amy and he makes her, her tea,
usually boiled spiders, sprinkled with bees.

amy's friend has his own special song,
but his singing is woeful and the intention is wrong.
he'll skip through the house with his pants on his head,
then they'll find him asleep on the roof of the shed.

The Shark Down The Toilet

Keith Beattie

There was a toilet many knew
Where you would never have to queue
For it was known beyond its dark
And shady U-bend hid a shark,
A fish of truly monstrous size
With tiny, piercing evil eyes,
And such a terrifying grin
That split his face from fin to fin.

This shark could squeeze his body whole
Right 'round the bend into the bowl
Where he would hide and wait all day
For any unsuspecting prey
To wander in and then begin
Their business unaware of him
Then he would pick their pockets bare
And hide the bog roll with great care.

Alas, one day he met his fate
This thieving shark awoke too late
To find he had been flushed away
Along the sewer, into the bay,
And there he got his just reward
And sat around all day, so bored
For he could make no fishy friends
Because he smelt of old U-bends.

Bedtime

Laura Robinson

At 8 o'clock before I go to bed
You can't imagine the things that go through my head.
The thought of monsters behind my curtain,
There was one last night, I'm almost certain.
The weird-looking shadows on my wall,
'It's only your imagination,' says my brother Paul.
But what does he know?
He lost his imagination long ago.

I know, I'll say my prayers then go to sleep
Surely then the monsters won't give a peep.
Ahhhhh! What was that out in the hall?
Oh, it's only my brother Paul.
Boy did he give me a scare,
For a minute there, I though he was a bear.

Right, I'll just calm down now and get some rest.
But all I can think of are those darn pests.
It's now 9 o'clock and Mum's gone to bed,
'Turn off the light and go to sleep,' that's what she said.
But it's all right for her, she's forty-four.
She doesn't think about monsters anymore.

I'm now quite tired; I think I'll sleep.
Maybe I'll try counting sheep.
Then in the morning, when the sun comes out,
I won't have to worry about the monsters about.

Waking Up

Louise McGibbon (15)

When the sun comes up
In the green countryside
And all the little birds
No longer hide,
For morning has come
And everything's awakening
Another day has started
And dawn is breaking.
The cows are turned out
Into the green, green pastures
The sun comes up
Faster and faster.
At the bottom of the lane
In a cottage named 'Plod',
A sleepy little head
Is wakening from the Land of Nod.
He rubs his eyes
And scratches his head,
Walks into the kitchen
Mmmm, his breakfast is made.
Boiled eggs and toast,
Tastes just right,
After a long sleep last night.
When breakfast is over,
He washes himself
Puts on his clothes,
He's like a little elf.
He gets to school
And plays quite loud,
But his mum is really proud.

Our Stepdad

Faye Berry (9)

You came into our lives that day.
You chased away our pain.
You took us on adventures.
And made Mammy smile again.

You do all things that daddies do,
You never made a fuss.
You just want to make us happy,
A little family, the four of us.

In the park we search for pouncers,
Become cowboys, Indians too,
You always make things fun for us,
That's just because you're you.

At night you keep us tucked up safe,
You shield us from all harm.
You chase away the monsters,
Make us laugh and keep us warm.

We love you like a real dad,
We agree, you've passed the test.
So we send you love and hugs and stuff,
'Cos you're simply 'the best'.

Rabbits

Ken Sainsbury

Isn't it a funny thing
We never hear a rabbit sing?
Sometimes, perhaps - a little squeak
But never more than once a week
With ears like that you can't go wrong
They *must* have heard the blackbird's song
And yet, although they're very cute
By and large they're almost mute
You will admit it would be great
When leaning on a country gate
To hear a bunny on the hop
Humming you the latest pop!
It really is a mystery
Why something quite so whiskery
Doesn't make a tuneful sound
But just makes big holes in the ground!

What's All The Fuss About Mum?

Ursula Fitzpatrick

Today's my first day, in this scary place
I think it's called school, I don't know a face.
Mum tells me it's fun, Dad says that it's great
please show me the door and open the gate.
I feel lost and small, alone and not sure
please let's go home and open the door.
A lady has come to take me to class
I don't want to go, I want to run fast.
Mum please, it's not fair, I shouldn't be here
I'm not ready yet, I'm so full of fear.
'See you,' you say and kiss me goodbye
a hug and a squeeze, so why do you cry?
is it that bad, it upsets you that much
why have you left me in such a rush?
As I look round and take in the view
I notice there's other kids just like me too.
All of us, stunned with our mouths wide, agape
please open the door and show us the gate.
Okay, we sit down and have a wee chat
the teacher is funny, I think I like that.
She laughs and she smiles and tells a joke too
is this all there is? Is this what we do?
It can't be that bad, after all it is three
and there I can see you waiting for me.

I've been here 2 months now and love it so much
I run through the doors, I can't get enough.
I've learned how to spell and to add 2+2
every day's different, I learn something new.
Don't be so sad Mum, what's happened to you?
I still love you heaps, but I love my school too.

The Haunted House

Marilyn Cliff

Through the dusty doorway,
up the darkened stairs,
I hear sounds of breathing
but there's no one there.

A cool draught hits my body,
I feel it crawl across my skin.
And still I hear the breathing
though I know there's no one in.

I grasp the brass door handle
that feels as cold as doom
then turn it very slowly
and go inside the room.

The air is damp and musty,
grey cobwebs shroud the light.
The breathing's very close now
so I scream with all my might.

My scream is like a siren
that stirs the rats and mice.
I slip on something nasty
which isn't very nice.

The breathing now is rasping
and harsh upon my ears.
I turn and run out, terrified
my mind is full of fears.
The door bangs shut behind me
and I'm outside on my own.
But still I hear the breathing
then an agonising groan.

For I've really been quite foolish
as it's now quite plain to see.
The source of that wild breathing
was not an *it* but *me!*

Spider On The Table

Pauline Somerset

A naughty little spider
Hanging from a tree,
A naughty little spider
Waved his legs at me.

'Good day,' I said, 'How are you?
I hope you've come to play.'
'Good day,' he said, 'That sounds like fun,
What a lovely day.'

He climbed down the tree trunk
And landed on my arm,
He crawled towards my open hand
And wriggled in my palm.

Mum was in the kitchen
Doing her last chore,
I closed my fingers carefully
And headed for the door.

I sat my new friend down
Upon the kitchen table
. . . The shrieks were heard all over town,
Mum's always been unstable.

I visit Mum in hospital
She's doing very well,
Dad says if I repeat the stunt
He'll make my life real hell!

Love For An Unseen Child

William Adam

I crave to paint my love for you,
With my artist loving hands.
And wrap you deep,
Within my woolly-cotton tenderness of father hood.

I lust to tell the knowledge,
Of what I could've been if . . . only if
My mother longs to love you,
Like the way she does of me.
But still we sit and watch the rain.

Like two sad children without innocence
Lost in the carnage of our heartache and the loss,
Wondering,
Your beauty is too much for our fragile egg shell world.

Shark

Sam Thornicroft (11)

A
Shadow slicker
Tail flicker
Flesh eater
Coral dweller
Seal pup smeller
Jaw snapper
Mouth gaper
Scale flapper
Shark!
He's a great white shark
Hunting in the sea
When he's calm, he's like
a mouse stealing all
the cheese
When he's mad, he's like a devil
with coal-black horns
Dashing through the water
As quickly as a dart
Into a fishing net
he swims
So fish he cannot eat
Slowly he droops his head
And slowly in the net he dies
As the net lifts
out of the water he
finds he cannot breathe

And seeing the
ocean where he once roamed
Deep blue and wavy
He died
His life was long
His life was scary
His life was full of eating and fighting.

The Ga Who Liked Dragons

Margaret Smith

I have a Ga. That's bad enough.
Other people have Grans or Nans
But she is a Ga. I called her Grandmother once.
She said that the last person who called her that
Was found at the bottom of a lime pit!
So now I always call her Grandmother -
When I don't think she is listening to me.

Anyway, she likes dragons. I ask you, dragons!
She collects them. There's nothing wrong with that.
Everyone collects something, stamps or teapots or mugs.
She has cupboards full - green china and purple glass
And smoothly, shiny metal, and ones with crystal eyes.

Which I could accept - if only she didn't believe in them.
Real dragons I mean - not shiny things to touch,
In cupboards or on walls. Yes, that's right, real ones!
You ought to hear her talk! She says dragons have had Bad Press,
And that St George was an interfering bully.

Of course she's mad - I mean - dragons!
I've tried to explain - but she only laughs!
I don't tell my friends of course, though I think they'd like her!
After all, she is different, I suppose,
Being a Ga! Not like a Nan or a Gran.
Dragons - huh! . . . I think I could put up with that,
But the only thing is, I wish, when I stay with her
She wouldn't let the biggest one - the one with shiny eyes
Eat all my cornflakes at breakfast!

Me Granny's On The Telly

Carolyn Bland

Me granny's on the telly.
Come quick and see.
She's had this urge
For fame and fortune.
It's way beyond me.

She's the tap-dancing granny
From down our street.
People won't believe
She's got tap-dancing feet.

She's dancing on the telly,
With energy untold.
We can't believe her nerve.
Because she's 84 years old.

Mum and Dad, come quickly!
Come quick and see!
Now we've told you once before Gran,
Get down off that TV!

The Things I See When I Go To Bed

Patricia Hunt

My mom said, 'It's all in your head'
The things you see when you go to bed.
I hate those words 'good night, sleep tight'
Because everything changes when they turn out the light.

What terrifies me, I can't really say
The things that frighten me at night,
I think, look real cool in the day.
Even though my room may look a sight.

Mom and Dad said I have a vivid imagination
But this one thing, I am absolutely certain
That my Action Man was playing, on the PlayStation.
Yet by morning, he was behind the bedroom curtain.

I try shutting my eyes, and going to sleep
But after a few moments, I've just got to take a peep
Because the things that go on in my room I'm sure,
Goes on in the room of the boy next door.

Soon daylight breaks, and a new day begins,
Every toy in their place and all the other things.
But I know this, that when it gets dark,
That's when all the strange things start.

The things I see, when I go to bed
Doesn't just happen to children you see.
Because most grown-ups have seen things too
When they were just as young as me!

Danny

Sue Wensley

Sleep on now, young Danny.
Like you, the sun has gone to bed,
But in the morning, the world will be ours.

Saturday tomorrow, Danny.
Juicy black berries waiting to be picked.
Fallen brown acorns asking to be collected.
Paper-thin sycamore wings for us to throw and fly.
Feather-weight leaves for us to gently crush.

Tomorrow, we can race across the lush green field,
Feeling the wind caressing our faces,
Dispelling the indoor cobwebs of the week.

Sleep on, Danny.
Rest your tired, young body now.
Tomorrow you will be fresh and free.
Free to feel the textures of the earth.
Free to see the vivid autumn colours.
Free to hear the songs of the birds, and the babble of human voices.
Tomorrow we shall enjoy life.

Your new wheelchair waits for you in the hall, Danny.
Shiny and bright; wheels awaiting movement.
Inviting you to a life of adventure.
Offering you exciting freedom.

Sleep on now, Danny.
Tomorrow we shall begin a lifetime of fun.

Sleep Tight!

Paul Burrell

'There's nothing as certain as this,' I said
To Mum, as she turned out the light,
'There's a crocodile under my bed now.
It's real, though it's not yet in sight.

It may appear shy but it's resting
And quietly waiting beneath.
For the moment I dangle one foot down
It will jump out and bite with its teeth.

Please Mother, why can't you believe me?
You just think I'm having you on,
But do understand that this creature
Is biding its time till you've gone.

And don't you go thinking I'm crazy
Or lost in a world of my own,
Since I know there's a risk of some wildlife
About in this house, still unknown.

I've heard wolves scratching round in the kitchen.
I know fruit bats hang under the stairs.
The dining room serves as a hideout
For a number of hungry brown bears.

The lounge is a room full of spiders,
Tarantulas lurk by the door.
Whilst the wardrobe's a site to avoid now,
Since I'm sure that I just heard a roar.

The bathroom's a place that I cannot abide.
The thought of it fills me with dread
Of snakes that reside in the plugholes
With piranhas which have not been fed.

So, putting my life in a nutshell . . .
Why don't I just stay here . . . in bed?'

I Wish . . .

Neil Bowden (6)

I wish I could fly a rocket
And go up to the moon
And see all the planets
And discover an ancient tomb
And if inside that ancient tomb
There was an ancient mummy
I'd run back to my rocket
Screaming *mummy mummy mummy.*

Flowers

Walter Botterill

The bright sun warms the good brown earth
as winter fades away
A bright green shoot comes creeping
to greet the light of day
Day by day the shoot creeps up
and spreads its leaves so green

First a swelling bud appears
to grace the plant so high
Then other buds come peeping
unfolding to the sky
Proud petals turn towards the sun
as spring and summer bloom

Colour bursts forth in radiant hue
to brighten up the gloom
The bees come dancing busily
so heavenly they jive

They sip the flowers' nectar sweet
to take off to their hive
The raindrops fall so prettily
sprinkling little showers
as they dance and slide so merrily
to freshen up the flowers.

The Skeleton, In A Box

M Lovesey

The skeleton that lives down below,
When you go past he'll say hello!
He'll raise his arms and shake his head,
And says hooray! I'm not dead,

He will rattle his bones and carry his chain,
Then he'll go running down the lane,
Where, he'll sit under a tree,
As you go by he'll wave to you and me,

He has no shoes, coat or hat
But one day he met a big black cat,
They chatted and laughed until the dawn,
Then went to sleep on a nice green lawn,

He says I'm so happy and jumps with glee,
Then he swung on the branch of a tree,
He sat on the riverbank
And paddled in the stream,
Then got back in his box
To slumber and dream.

Sister Under The Skin

Natalie Cook

My baby sister's very small,
All curled up in a tiny ball.
She has no toys. She wears no clothes,
Just sits and fiddles with her toes.

But she can hear and smell and feel,
Even though she's not yet real.
And when I tap my mummy's bump,
She answers with a little thump.

Then at the clinic, on the screen,
The sweetest thing I've ever seen!
The baby that she'll one day be
Sucks her thumb - just like *me!*

Later, when we have a nap,
Two heads rest in mummy's lap.
Sweet memories drift us off to sleep,
And two heads dream of when we'll meet.

Owl-Wise

Jill Roberts

What good am I, an owl with no hoots?
I usually store then next to my boots,
But after my preening and dressing this evening
I fluffed up my breast, to give of my best,
To stir the tired night, and had such a fright - nothing happened!

I tried again and again, for I did believe,
Hoots may be hidden up folds in my sleeve
So, drawing in air and puffing my chest,
Although quite exhausted, I could not rest,
With feet clutching branch, I stood my full height,
Preparing myself to farewell the night,
But only succeeded in trembling my plight - nothing happened!

Oh, what can I do now?
I'm sad and dismayed
It's terribly awkward when hoots are mislaid,
For unless they are trod on, or drop on the ground,
They can lie undiscovered without making a sound
So, there seems only one course I now have to follow,
To spring clean, in winter, my deciduous hollow,
For without my own note I am incomplete,
I must thoroughly search before facing defeat.

I've quivered the curtains and pulled up the rugs,
Shook all the bedclothes and upturned all jugs
Cleaned behind pictures, swept up the floor,
A quick cup of tea, then I'll work on some more.

As the kettle sits boiling, my head spins around,
For, instead of a whistle, I hear a strange sound,
And there, on its spout, my 'hoot' I have found!

How silly am I,
Thoughts come to me now,
I do remember, how I made a vow,
When kettle was dropped and whistle was bent,
Whilst repairs could take place, my 'hoot' I had lent.

Oh, what joy, what delight,
Now, I 'hoot' you 'Goooodnight!'

When I'm Needed

Heléna Cox
(Dedicated to my grandchildren)

Just think of me and I am there
To brush away deep fears.
I'll be your guardian angel,
Walk beside you through the years.
When you're alone I'll take your hand,
Gently guide you through the day.
In your sleepless nights I'll hold you tight,
Listen to what you say.
I'll be beside you in all you do,
Dry the teardrops that you cry.
When you're at your lowest ebb,
I'll lift your spirits high.
But when the need has lessened,
You're feeling good and strong,
Once again I'll slip away,
Content in knowing nothing's wrong.

Spacecycle

Sheila Freegard

I thought I saw a UFO flying in the sky
I'm sure I saw a Martian wave as he flew by
I was only on my pushbike, and then I hit a ramp
As I went hurtling into space, my armpits felt quite damp.
The Martian put his head out and told me to keep calm,
But the speed that I was travelling at caused me great alarm.
As I went peddling around and about and in and out of stars,
My front wheel buckled slightly and I crashed head on with Mars.
Exactly like a pinball I bounced from Mars to Saturn
I've never been so glad my mother made me put my hat on.
The earth was turning circles and I braced myself to land.
I hoped that I would fall on some nice, white fluffy sand.
I didn't know which way to turn; I looked around in fear,
And then I saw that Martian with a parachute quite near.
He waved the silk, gave me a smile, he nodded then a wink
And before you could say Jupiter down to earth I began to sink.
I don't know how I did it, I can't say any more
But do you know where I landed, right on my bedroom floor
It couldn't be a dream; I know it was quite real
I've examine all the evidence and changed my bike's front wheel.

A Great Big Mouth

B Colebourn

I'm just a great big mouth,
That's circled by two lips;
Who loves to burp out loud,
When stuffed with fish and chips!
Sometimes I'm even burnt,
When hot liquid passes through;
It causes such annoyance,
Especially when I've flu!
Sometimes I feel so bloated,
From all that I have chewed;
But the more I do object,
The more I'm stuffed with food!

The only rest I get,
Is when I'm feeling sore;
Which is when I throw my weight around,
By spewing on the floor!

Christmas Day

Valerie Harris

It's Christmas Day
and I'm wide awake,
I want to get up,
I just can't wait!

So I creep downstairs,
and what do I see?
a million presents,
under the tree!

I think I'll touch,
or squeeze, or see,
if there's just one
that's meant for me!

The paper is crisp,
the ribbon all curly,
I can hardly see though,
It must be very early.

I quickly rip the paper,
and just about peep inside,
when suddenly the light goes on,
and mum shouts 'It's only half past five!'

Tears In The Sand

Suzanne Marcuslee

Angels waiting silently . . . outside God's Promised Land, to
Greet these unfortunate Sudanese children . . . with a
Loving hand. For an eternal Life of loving . . . in the
Heavens . . . flowing with milk and honey, where innocence is
More valuable . . . than food . . . water or money.

Born out of love . . . into a once green and opulent
Pasture, now devoid of vegetation . . . as the mid-day
Sun . . . robs them of a future. Tears of pain and
Hunger . . . increasing with every passing day, comforted by
Their starving parents . . . as their lives ebb away.

Tribal warfare continues . . . despite the nation's grief,
Preventing the distribution . . . of much needed food
Relief. A once proud nation in turmoil . . . overcome with a
Pestilence of greed, thus starving these little hearts
Of pure gold . . . of the nourishment they need.

As the scorching Middle East sun rises . . . into a crystal
Clear blue sky, thousands of starving children . . . whimper
. . . groan and cry. Hunger etched on their little faces
. . . bones visible beneath their withered skin, as
Another day of horrendous torment . . . needlessly sets in.

Babies and infants . . . suckling at their mothers' barren
Breast, unaware of their impending doom . . . and the
Approaching final test. Tears evaporating on the parched
Sand . . . beneath the merciless sky, as their parents impart
A tender kiss . . . and bid them a sorrowful goodbye.

Emergency food supplies arriving . . . too little . . . too
Late, as thousands of little souls . . . depart on their
Journey . . . to The Pearly Gate. Embraced by God's angels
Under a shroud of heavenly loving care, as their tears on
The sand become a forgotten memory . . . along with the pain
They had to bear.

The Firework Display

Patrick McCluskey

The firework display.
The heavens explode
And kaleidoscopic
Flashes of brilliance
Transfix childmind eyes.
Pupils, start to dilate,
As heartbeats grow
Ever so fast
From the thunderous applause.
Up above, bright sparks fade,
And jaws p
     l
     u
     n
     g
     e
In he semi-darkness.
Then, out-of-the-blue,
The sky lights up
A terrific splash of colour,
Sending children screaming
For more . . .
But the night rolls on,
And eyes, laden with sleep,
Walk silently to slumber

To dream . . . ah to zzzzz.

School Dinners

Andrew Duggan

It comes to you in an awful state,
you must stop it walking off your plate.
The meat I think is still alive,
it jumped at me and I had to dive.
That green stuff just doesn't look right,
the potatoes belong on a building site.
I slowly put it in my mouth
and before it began its journey south,
I tell no lie, it's the truth,
that Brussel sprout chipped my tooth.
It really was a familiar taste,
it reminded me of toxic waste.
I had to finish, I could take no more,
eating that stuff made my mouth sore.
I was always told wasting food is a sin,
but that stuff belongs in the bin.
The dinner lady comes from Mars,
for feeding us that, she belongs behind bars.
Her face is wrinkled and she wears a wig,
That stuff she makes would poison a pig.
It's hard to believe she's someone's wife,
When she looks at you, you run for your life.

Ashleigh's Sunflowers

A Simpson

Come along to Ashleigh's garden,
Colourful the whole year round.
She grows plants and shrubs for pleasure,
All sorts of flowers can be found.

'My garden looks so small this springtime.
What it needs is something high,'
Sighed Ashleigh one sunny morning.
'I know, a sunflower as tall as I!'

So she planted tiny seedlings,
Watered them and watched them grow.
Quickly they grew all through the summer,
Till one day she cried, 'Oh no!'

The sunflowers had grown and grown,
As high as rooftops, or so it seemed.
Her daddy gasped, her mummy fainted,
But her next-door neighbour screamed!

'What on earth are they you're growing,
In your garden, by the fence?
They are blocking all my sunshine.
You must cut them down . . . or else!'

Ashleigh's eyes were filled with tears,
When she heard the neighbour's pleas.
'But what about my golden sunflowers
And those twenty bumblebees?'

Her neighbour watched her face with sadness
And she had a change of tune.
'Oh, all right then, you may keep them,
If you grow bluebells next June!'

Our Very Own

June Cooper

Hey stop! Look down! That's right, I'm here!
I've just been born, I'm full of cheer!

What are you though? It's hard to see!
An oak, or ash? What kind of tree?
Perhaps it's a bluebell, or daffodil.
A crocus maybe? No, it's far too chill.

Hey stop! Look now! I've grown some more.
While you were talking I grew I'm sure!

Were you a pip? A sycamore wing?
A hazelnut? How did you begin?

I fell from that tree . . . the one over there.
So that's who I am! Why do you stare?

Well, that's the King of all the trees!
So you are a Prince, may we serve you, please?

I'm very small and rather shy.
Do you mean one day I'll touch the sky?

It all depends; it's very hard.
In winter storms you'll need some guard.
Perhaps we could build a stony wall.
Protect you from the dangers that fall.

Oh that is nice, you're very kind.
Are you quite sure you wouldn't mind?

A sapling needs a helping hand.
You'll be *our tree,* this is Your Land.
Fetch little stones, but leave some light.
A marker now to measure height.

And every day we'll chart your growth.
And water you well . . . We need a post!

We've found a tree, our very own.
We'll take great care until you've grown.
Maybe, one day, in years to come,
Our children will play here, like us, in the sun.

Deceit

Robert E Fraser

The frog sat on the lilypad
Floating on the mere
Croaking in the falling rain
'Sweet damsel fly come near,
Come listen to my lonely song
And hear my sad refrain,
My legs have gone quite funny
And I'll never jump again!'

The damsel fly in hovered flight
Said 'Do you feel much pain?
Your colour is quite green you know,
Green as bamboo cane
I'll come a little closer
To have a better scan'
A sticky tongue flicked the air
And the damsel fly had gone.

Ode To Bedtime

Vivvi

Well, here we are, bedtime again - let's have a little fun.
I'll read awhile till you drop off, you're such a lovely son.
I love this time, just you and me, I love to read to you,
The very old books we've read and read, and those that are still new.

It's funny though, it always seems you choose a book that's long -
With heaps of pages and loads of chapters and sometimes
there's a song!
I'll read and sing . . . and sing and read, but you just don't get tired,
An hour passes by so quick and a headache I've acquired!

'Let's have a drink and chocolate bar' you ask me just by chance.
'Alright,' I say, although I think you're leading me a dance!
We get all cosy on the bed, the tuck is on a plate,
'What's going on?' I ask myself - it's getting rather late.

Another story, another rhyme, you're very much awake!
I love you dear, but feel that there's not much more I can take!
You tell me you don't want no more of your mate Postman Pat,
But then you sit up in your bed and feel sorry for Jess the cat!

My patience is thin, my nerves are shot, the time is ticking by,
'You've no intentions of closing your eyes,' I say to myself with a
sigh!
But wait, I've found this book on your top shelf about some sheep,
It's all to do with counting them whilst going off to sleep!

Well, what a find, why hadn't I come across this book before?
It won't be long before your eyelids drop to sleep I'm sure.
It's all gone quiet, I do believe you've laid your head to rest -
Goodnight, sweetheart, I love you loads, a kiss to say God Bless!

Autumn Fairies

Marilyn Lamond

September and October are the months the fairies come,
And if you don't believe me then just go and ask your mum.

At first their toadstool dwellings will emerge from underground,
They build them and make villages, you scarcely hear a sound.

For food they gather berries which they find on bush and tree,
There's blackberries, crab-apples, sloes - a tad too sour for me.

What I find fascinating, is the clothing that they wear,
They weave the finest fabrics which will float as light as air.

The silk worms and the spiders, they provide this fairy thread,
The fairies make their garments thus to cover toe to head.

What are these fairies doing while they're here for this short time?
They make the autumn magical and some might say sublime.

They sprinkle dust into the sky to make the sunsets glow,
The red-gold sunbeams radiate and touch the trees, you know.

They count the stars and have to check each heav'nly constellation
And by the starlight they continue fairy operations.

The petals and the leaves begin to fall upon the ground
And fairies whisk them clean away with just a rustling sound.

They send to Mother Nature all those things which fall and die.
They know that Mother Nature will re-cycle by-and-by.

The fairies ride on butterflies and furry bumblebees.
They also live inside the blossoms growing on some trees.

In certain flower petals they are known to hide their shoes,
For I have seen their footwear, which they really hate to lose.

The fairies come and visit you if you should lose a tooth,
They pay you for your 'pearlies' and that is the honest truth.

The fairies help you find the things that took themselves astray.
They're everywhere around you and no matter where you play.

So when you find some toadstool rings, please do not squash them flat,
The fairies live there for a while - now what d'you think of that?

Tea With Great-Grandma

Nicky Adams

I sleep tight on Sunday nights,
so tired and really weary,
as Sunday afternoons are spent
with great-grandma, bright and cheery.
We hear her knock at three o'clock
and rush to take her bags,
kisses all round as she sits down,
the sofa badly sags.

She always has two biscuits,
a bun and then a crumpet,
she drains her teacup, puts it down
and then out comes the trumpet.
She toots us all a little tune,
wolfs down a sausage roll,
then someone shouts 'kick-about!'
- great-grandma plays in goal.

Back in for a cheese sandwich
and a rest in the armchair,
but then she finds her stripey bag
- we know what she keeps in there.
With elbows flying all around,
great-grandma's just a blur,
accompanied by a rustling sound,
a noisy clack and whirr.

Her glasses glint, her fillings flash,
her curls bounce and collide,
the windows shake, the teacups quake,
the dog runs off to hide.
In a while she starts to slow,
she sighs and says 'It's ready.'
Good old great-grandma's knitted me
a jumper for my teddy!

There's Always

Janet Dougherty

There's always tomatoes in your sick.
There's always greenies from your nose to pick.
There's always runny farts to blow.
Ask my mate, he should know!

There's always the gobstoppers you saved from last year.
There's always the finger to suck when you've dug out your ear.
And don't forget the greenies if you're pickin'
You know they're always 'finger lickin'?

And a few little skid marks in your pants.
Has got to be better than pants full of ants.
There's always crusty scabs to pick.
Pick 'em near girls till they're feeling sick.

Then suck the blood till those girls turn white.
Then ask for a kiss, you know that's right.
then burp in their faces instead of kissin'
Lovely stuff, they don't know what they're missin'!'

And there's always practising burps and farts.
'Cos there's always time for your 'finer arts'!

Robot Man

Marilyn Davidson

Tom was a little robot
Man
Who walked across the
Floor

All the children screamed
And laughed
They wanted to see more

His suit was all shiny
And he had a little gun

He had a smile across
His face
The children thought was
Fun

On his feet were moving
Wheels
Along the floor they
Squeaked and squealed

A little light inside his
Chest
He really looked the very
Best

He fired his little laser
Gun up and all around
And when his batteries
Ran out
He fell upon the ground

The Snowman

C Metcalfe

When it snows, children know that they can
Turn the snow, into their own snowman
A big snowball, its body will make
For its head, a smaller one it will take

And on the head, he will need a face
Made of coal and a carrot, they will place
He will wear a scarf and hat, and he won't fuss
And in his hand, they will place a brush

He will stand outside all night, and it will freeze
But from him, there will be no cough or sneeze
Because the snowman, no cold can be felt
If he gets warm, then he will surely melt.

Time For Bed

Stephanie Kate Brooks

The sky's gone dark, the stars are out
It's time for bed, Mum begins to shout

I roll my eyes, beg and plead
For five more minutes, but I don't succeed

I brush my teeth, and comb my hair
Dad tucks me in tight, with my teddy bear

A kiss on each cheek, and the lights go out
My eyelids are heavy, I'm out for the count

Bye, bye my world, thanks for all you do
Let my dreams be filled with wonderful things - mums
and dads too!

It Wuz 'Im

Kathy Birkitt

Oi can't 'elp it . . .
Oi saw 'im
'e pushed 'im
Then 'e pushed me
Din ya see 'im Miss?

No oi din 'it 'im - 'onest!
'e's always cauzin' trouble Miss
An' blamin' uvver people . . .
In't fair!
Las' week 'e 'it our teacher an'
She wuz in a terrible state
Cryin', red face
Such a tizz
But Mr Medd our 'ed
Sorted 'im out
An' sent for 'is muvver.
She went mad
An' walloped 'im
Gurd!
'e deserved it.
Nuvver time, Miss, 'e frew 'is dinner
at the dinner lady,
Ya shurd 'av seen 'er face
Covered in beans an' potato . . .
Talk 'bout mad!
'e nearly got expelled Miss
Pidy 'e din.

Oi din do that Miss
'e pushed by an' knocked the paint pots
On the floor
Oi saw 'im
'e did it purposely Miss, 'e wanted to get me inta
trouble
An' now there's paint everywhere
An' all over moi lovely work!
Yes it was gurd Toyah . . .
Moi picture was really gurd,
Better than yours!
In fact oi fink it wuz you
Who pushed yer chair back
An' tripped 'im up.
It wuzn't me Miss 'onest
'e's always cauzin' trouble!

At the end of school Miss
'e went inta the cloakroom
An' frew all the coats in a 'eap
An' jumped on 'um all
Oi saw 'im
'e kicked the lunchboxes 'round too
An' at least free opened up . . .
'ec of a mess Miss!
Mr Medd saw it
But oi said
It wuzn't me sir . . .
Oi din do it
It wuz 'im
'e's always cauzin' trouble!

Ickleland

Sharon Ward

The trees are tall in Ickleland
the sky is always blue,
the fluffy clouds are candyfloss,
and the sun always shines through.

The rain falls lightly in Ickleland,
and children always play,
all the houses are made of candy,
and pets, they never stray.

Time does not exist in Ickleland,
so rest your dainty head,
happiness reigns forever,
and tears are never shed.

Monsters and nasties are banished from Ickleland,
they cannot breathe the air,
the purity is far too much,
for evil kind to bear.

Each rainbow is within the reach,
of every tiny hand,
and when you've felt the colours there,
you'll know you've been to Ickleland.

Whichford Woods

Stuart Kershaw

A thousand flowers it seems I can see
The butterflies dance with delight,
Feeding upon the nectar rich source
Until the dark, of night;

The only sound to break the silence
Is the song of the birds as they sing with glee,
A perfect calm on a perfect day
This is the life for me;

I hear the call of a buzzard above
Gliding with effortless ease,
No doubt surveying what is his patch
For prey to tempt and tease.

Beneath a beech tree there stands a headstone
To mark the grave of a man's best friend,
A favourite place they could call their own
Until the very end.

Dogs

Janet Lambert

I like dogs they're wonderful creatures,
tongues lolling, eyes gleaming,
creating happy features.
Coming home from shopping
they're there to meet you at the door,
flopping over on their backs
squirming on the floor.
Soft wet noses nuzzle you as you
unpack the bag,
Mum always brings us something
back, their tails begin to wag.
Soft brown eyes rest on mine,
yes I think dogs were meant
to make man's life peaceful,
blissful and content.

Midnight Star

Jayne Moore

Goodnight, goodnight, my sleepyhead
It's time to say 'Au revoir'
I lay you down upon your bed
To watch the midnight star

The star appears as it grows dark
And yet it glows so bright
So beautiful a jewel can shine
Only in cloudless night

A myriad of sister stars
Surround her, in a throng
They seem to sing in harmony
To her melodic song.

So crystal clear, her glory shines
And twinkles through the gloom
Her silver light will shimmer
And illuminate this room

So close your eyes my darling child
Be cosy in your bed
And as you curl up, nice and warm,
The stars are overhead

Albeit dark, there's always light
Around us on the earth
When daylight dies and it grows dark
The stars are given birth.

The Baby Boy

F Burton

Six years have passed by,
I cannot imagine where they have gone
No matter how I try
When I looked upon a baby boy.

He looked so lovely lying there
With velvety skin that was so fair
Jet black hair and eyes of blue
That seemed to say 'Who are you?'

Each day brought joy to Dad and Mum
Watching him kick and smile
Holding him was so much fun
Making everything seem worthwhile.

Soon he was bouncing up and down
Enjoying every minute
Soon on the floor he started creeping
Next he was peacefully sleeping.

What excitement the day brought
When he began to walk and talk
The joy that was shared with so much love
Must have been sent from heaven above.

Like most boys he gets very naughty
Making Dad and Mum begin to worry
Then, after a while he says 'I'm sorry.'

He now has reached the age of six
Full of life and childish tricks
Dad and Mum's pride and joy
Still their darling little boy.

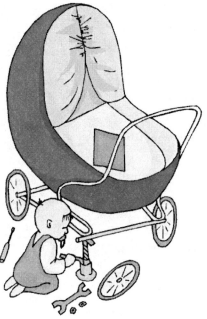

There's A Baby Coming!

Angie Slade

There's a baby coming
I'm sure about that,
I've seen the cradle
and the changing mat.

What's going on?
What about me?
I'm still a baby
I'm not even three!
I'm still learning to
hop, skip and jump
and what does Mum do?
Grow a great bump.

Is that where it's hiding?
I really don't care
It must be quite stupid
to hide under there!

Still it's only a baby
I shouldn't really shout
I mean after all

How's it gonna get out?

Animals In Summer

Anna-Marie Treloar

Sheep in the shade,
Out of the sun,
The lambs don't mind,
They just have fun.

Children in the garden,
Being watched by dog,
Ants crawling round the garden,
Log to log.

Hedgehogs and foxes,
Out at night,
Owls and their babies,
In the pale moonlight.

Animals and plants,
Growing each day,
It's summer now,
Hip hip hooray!

Simon Scallywag

J P C Ludford

Simon Scallywag was weird,
Or so it seemed when he appeared.
His hat was made of candyfloss.
His coat was green and made from moss.
His shirt was made from bits of tin.
Which sometimes scratched his neck or chin.
His trousers were of bamboo cane,
Which kept out wind, sleet, snow and rain.
His cobweb socks were strong as steel,
With spiders clinging to the heel.
His shoes were buckets made from peat,
And were too large for his small feet.
He had long nails to scratch his toes,
A tea cosy covered his nose.
He washed his clothes in desert sand,
With wooden gloves on either hand.
He spoke a language no one knew,
And loved to eat banana stew.
He always took his breakfast late,
Of frozen porridge on a slate.
He sipped on seaweed tea at night,
To make him dream without a fright.
So Simon Scallywag was weird,
Or so it seemed when he appeared.

Crocodile Surprise

Trish Duxbury

If you go to Africa and wander on the plains
You'll see cheetahs, lions and elephants -
(just to mention a few names!)
Not forgetting zebras and the poor old wildebeest,
who often gives the lioness and her cubs a feast!
And walking through the jungle
You'll see monkeys in the trees
Snakes, frogs and lizards -
And much, much more than these!
Many kinds of spiders, exotic birds and bees
And though I haven't seen them
There must be jungle fleas!
A dirty, muddy waterhole
Take a look and you will find
An enormous hippopotamus -
A pachyderm or thick-skinned kind!
Two glistening rows of large, white teeth
Jaws gaping open wide
Snap! the crocodile has got you!
Tell me, is it dark inside?

Detention

Lisa Tweddle (12)

I was in my first ever Spanish lesson,
the teacher began to talk
I hadn't a clue what she was saying
So my mind began to walk.

20 minutes later the teacher asked me a question,
I couldn't give her an answer
So, her next words were
Detention!

Spider's Second Attempt

Benderetti

'Can my treacle tarts not tempt you?'
Said the spider to the fly,
For you've surely smelt them cooking
As you were passing by.
Come and look around my house
Humble though we are,
Come and rest yourself awhile
For I know you've travelled far.

Talk to me pretty one.'
Said the spider to the fly.
'You flatter me.' the fly returned.
Said the spider, 'No, not I.'
'I merely tell you what I see
And what I say is true;
It delights me, lovely creature
To cast my sight on you.

So come into my house, dear heart,
Let my words caress you for a while;
Rest those lovely legs
Do not walk another mile.
Does my silvered speech persuade you?'
Said the spider to the fly;
'When flies are dinner to a spider?'
Said the other, 'No, not I.'

Wishes

Bill Sutherland

If I had a fairy godmother,
Who said she would grant all I wish,
I think that the list I would give her,
Would probably read just like this.

I *wish* that I was able to fly,
And soar with the birds way up in the sky,
I'd look down on mountains
And fly over the sea, and only go home
When called in for tea.
I *wish* I could swim in the ocean,
Search for treasures under the sea,
And swim with the whales and the dolphins
How exciting all that would be.
I *wish* I could dance in the ballet,
I'd twirl and leap all around the floor,
The people would clap hands together
Then stand on their feet and cry 'More'
I *wish* I could be a great singer,
And sing songs from morning till night
I'd start after breakfast each morning,
And stop before supper each night.
I *wish* I could drive my own little car,
And visit my friends, whether near or afar,
I'd zoom down the motorway
Perhaps stopping once,
To put in some petrol and stretch all my joints.

Though I may not be granted all wishes,
My main wish has come true, you see,
Long ago Mom and Dad chose a little girl,
And the little girl chosen . . . was me.

Babysitter

D M Harrington

I wanted a brother called George
But no one listened to me
They showed me a little bundle
Saying, 'You'll like her, you'll see.'

What can I do with a sister?
She can't play football with me
My friends would laugh and titter
They wouldn't play with me.

If I had a brother called George
Which I did order, after all,
We could play rough games
And never tire at all.

I suppose I am stuck with a sister
And really, she's not too bad,
Perhaps I'll learn to love her

And let her play in my pad!

The Wizard Of The Well

Glen Thomas

Many, many years ago
This tale was one that I heard tell
Of a rare, good wizard, who lived by a well.

He was kind and the children would him seek
With moss green clothes and foam-white hair
- Bright blue eyes and ruddy cheeks.
Often, I heard tell
He would whistle, gently, down the well
The people round about thought him odd
But he was helpful too, as he lived near
Would draw the water for the children
Every bucketful, sparkling, cool and clear.

Then some strange folk came to the well to drink
And drove him away, without pause to think
He stood a distance off, with blazing eyes, cheeks so ruddy
And every bucketful raised by those wicked folk
Was still, dark and very muddy.

That was long ago, there are few wells now
Instead we have large lakes and reservoirs
It is said the wizards, all, are gone,
But on some nights, you can still hear
Among the trees around the lakes
- A gentle whistling sound
And there is no wizard standing near
But how then, can we be sure
When every glass, drawn from your tap
Is sparkling, cool and clear.

Christine Henshaw (11)

Now that I'm at senior school,
I really think it's kind of cool,
To make new friends and teachers too,
Who are there to teach me and you,
Now I have written this poem just to say,
How I felt on my first day.
A little nervous on the inside, happy on the out,
I thought it was time to learn what school was all about.
Moving round the corridors, trying to find my way,
Was very difficult at first, this I have to say.
After being here two weeks, I don't find it too hard,
To seek which room where I have to be,
Whether it's room one to fifty three.
Lessons are over, the day is done,
The bell rings, it's time to have fun.

Childhood Joy

Ada Pickering

Come, my dear children, hasten to play,
The sun shines so brightly, 'tis a beautiful day
Take a trip to the park, sing like a lark,
Round the trees run and dance, make your feet prance,
How happy you'll be, as older faces you see,
Shine with faces, as bright as the sun,
As they watch children play, so happy and gay,
Oh they really are having such fun,
Then for a treat, on the grass take a seat,
Share a picnic, we all will partake,
Sandwiches, crisps, fizzy pop,
Mummy's iced cakes with a cherry on top,
Soon homeward we go, for it's bedtime you know,
Gaily, we run round the bends,
Waving goodnight to our friends,
Say 'Thank you, Mum,' give her a big hug,
As gently, she tucks us in bed,
Now, we are warm and snug,
We hear her voice say, at the end of the day,
'Sleep well, goodnight, and God bless. I love you.'

Hallowe'en

Lauren McGarrity

Hallowe'en will be here soon,
All the ghosts and witches will be out,
Just watch when you're out and about.

Sucking blood and biting necks
Vampires fly about in the night
There are also mummies
Wrapped so tight.

So be careful when you're out at night
This poem could be right.

Blast-Off

Frankie Illingworth (8)

Ten!
I really want to do it!
Nine!
I wonder what it's like in space?
Eight!
It's going to be fun!
Seven!
I wonder what the food's like?
Six!
I hope I don't get sick!
Five!
I hope the engine works!
Four!
I don't want to do it!
Three!
I hope I don't die!
Two!
I don't want to go!
One!
Help!

Ode To A 3 Year Old

Helen Darlington

Pure as a snowflake
Busy as a bee
Strong as a snowdrop
Drawing life from you and me.

Gentle as a moonbeam
Warmer than the sun
Pleasing as a little fawn
Learning how to run.

Frightened as a centipede
Hiding behind stones
But brave as a mirror
Accepting any life it is shown.

Michael

A Craig

Michael Craig is my little lad.
I don't think there's a day
When he's ever been bad.
He helps in the house and he tidies the toys
and I can't say that about some other boys.
He's brilliant at science, and excellent in maths
and you want to see him swim at the baths.
He keeps winning this and he keeps winning that,
he's top in all exams that he's ever sat.
The teachers all love him reading a book,
it won't be long now, he'll be learning to cook!
He's happy in school and he's got loads of friends,
if anything's broken he'll just make amends.
His writing and spelling are brilliant too,
I don't think there's much that this boy can't do.
A beautiful face and those great big brown eyes,
he doesn't steal money and doesn't tell lies.
Basketball, football, he plays any game,
when friends throw a party they're all glad he came.
There's one thing I'll say now, that I'm really glad
he's my little son 'cos I love him like mad. . .

Mum

Bright Sun

Barbara Ann Fields

Bright sun, summer's day
Off to the seaside for the day
Costumes packed, buckets and spades too
Lots of fun for you and me
Look, look there's the sea and oh!
Look, rocks as well . . .
Waves dance here and there
Sand is warm beneath our feet
Rocks, rocks everywhere
Share your secrets large and small
Magic ponds and tiny crabs
Sea anemones an oh! Look, look
A tiny movement
A sparkle of light
A rock fairy dances into sight
Closer, closer bending down
I watch as she bathes and plays
Another small figure and yet one more
What magic do these rocks unfold?
Jumping on crabs and climbing seaweed
Tiny laughter reaches my ears
The tide draws nearer to greet the rocks
Do not despair when it is high
They have their secret place to hide.

To Be Or Not To Be - With Bianca

Chrissie Panter

I wish I could get a part, in one of Gran's favourite soaps
Like Toyah's boyfriend in *Corrie* or dishy Leanne's, some hopes . .

I'd bash that dozy Spider, and bewilder his nice Auntie Em
Then take on Curly and Tyrone, prove I'm not scared of them.

In *Eastenders* the Di Marco brothers would quake as I walk past
To convince their sultry sister Teresa, he Mr Right is here at last.
Though Sarah Hills is sweet, she's a little too easy to shock
I'd play it by ear, and serenade this one with Gospel Rock.

We only watch *Emmerdale* when my gran needs a
                                        breath of fresh air . . .
Jack Sugden's fine on the farm, but he neglects his wife's loving care
All stunners in their swimsuits, are the girls from Summer Bay,
But Irene is such a foghorn, I may feel safer at home than away.

No homework done - again, so I got into big trouble at school
'Not good enough, Ricky,' Sir frowned 'especially as
                                        you're no fool . . .
Write five hundred lines, on the subject of *Women at War*
Your gran lets you watch too much TV, as I've mentioned
                                        to her before.'

I *won't* write about Boadicea, chariots are dead boring, I think . . .
Nor Cleopatra, though an asp drove this beauty to the brink.
I dig modern feuds, like Bianca's and Carol's over big Dan . . .
Delicious freckled Bee, call me *'Rick-kay!'* as only you can.

Next to Bee, policeman Angie's scrap with Mandy in her fur . . .
But writing about soap heroines probably won't wash with Sir.

Dream Sweet Dreams

Benita McNamee

Goodnight my little angel,
You're tired now, go to sleep,
While Mummy reads a bedtime tale
Rest now, try not to peep.

Because Mrs Sun is sleeping,
Mr Moon is out to play,
So close your eyes and rest awhile
Until another day.

Dream sweet dreams my darling,
While you're tucked up safe in bed,
Sleep while Mr Sandman sings
And rest your little head.

Let angels sleep beside you,
And guide you through the night,
Until the stars all disappear
Until the morning light.

Untitled

Melanie Havelock

Now close your eyes
But don't you cry
'Cause Mummy's here by your side
I'll tuck you in
I'll say goodnight
And then turn off your golden light.

And when I do,
Don't fear, don't sigh
'Cause Mummy's only just outside,
I'll read you this
And hope as planned
You'll soon be off to Slumberland.

Match Of The Day

Ann Priestley

King Lion, one day, said his zoo team would play,
At football, a team from Great Britain
Whose team from the wild, of shy creatures mild
Were afraid they would be badly bitten.
Two tigers up front left a pig just to grunt
The zebras made wild hares look slow.
A lolloping leopard found a sheep with no shepherd
Had no idea which way to go.
A giraffe at the back stopped every attack
That the country team's small players made.
A fast-moving cheetah ran the wing - every metre -
Leaving badgers and foxes dismayed.
But the zoo team's gorilla, as strong as Godzilla,
Could not get his side to score first
Each time their shots stole near the hedgehog in goal
The ball hit his prickles and burst.
It looked like a draw, with no one to score
Till a tiny, young, velvet-skinned mole
With a burrowing bound drove the ball underground
And popped up again in the goal.
The shocked goalie's cough blew his football shorts off
And his trunk knocked the referee flat
But the short-sighted owl would not give a foul,
He said 'It's a goal and that's that!'
So the small creatures won, they'd had lots of fun,
At football they'd beaten the rest.
From jungle or zoo it's still very true
You needn't be big to be best.

Babba-Monster

Paul Holland

He is the *Babba-monster* and his skin was putrid brown,
He is the *Babba-monster* and he always wore a gown
Of vomit green and doo-doo red,
An orange helmet on his head;

So listen now to what is said:
He hides beneath my fluffy bed;
In the shadow of my duvet's fall
Lies the *Babba-monster*, eight feet tall.
With shoes of bogey-black patent leather
And trousers - *wowzers*! I don't know whether
Or not I can say of the snot they are made.
The best I can do is a mucus-blue suede.

He is the *Babba-monster* and he had not a friend
He is the *Babba-monster*; a disgusting blend
Of insipid odour and foul, rotten colours,
But he needed a home under my covers
And I gave him that shelter because he's my mate;
He helps with my school work and stays up till late.

The Unicorn And The Dragon

R Marr

The unicorn was walking along the country lane,
When suddenly the sky darkened and it began to rain,
The unicorn said 'Gosh, this rain is coming down helter-skelter
I think I'd better look around, and try to find some shelter.'
A cave in a hillside, he saw was close nearby
He thought 'I'll go in there and in it I'll keep quite dry.

The cave was spacious, wide and tall, almost like a mini hall,
When from the back of it he heard some one his name call.
'Percy Unicorn!' The voice repeated yet again
Then a puff of smoke, passed him like an express train.
He rounded a corner, and there to his great surprise
Was Robbie Dragon wiping tears from his weeping eyes.

'What ails thee, Robbie?' Said Percy with great concern,
Trying to avoid the dragon's spouting flames in turn.
Which into ashes threatened him to burn.
''Tis that gallant knight, Saint George' the dragon said
'All day he's chased me hither and thither
Till he's fair got me dizzy, and I'm in an awful dither.'

'Aye, Robbie,' Percy Unicorn said, 'I know just how you feel,
For whole nations have been seeking me to see if I am real.
Even the horn from my head they would take,
And with it magic potions they would make.
If only some secret land we could both find,
And live out our lives with creatures of our own kind.'

'Look Percy!' Robbie said, 'This cave goes back an awful long way,
And right at the back I can see the light of day,
But being by myself, I have always been afraid to go,
For I've never been a brave dragon as well you know.
But with you close at hand I know I can make a stand.'
And so together they advanced into an unknown land.

From the cave they emerged into the strange land,
To find creatures of their own kind near at hand,
Robbie Dragon gave vent with such a great roar of delight,
That the cave shook then collapsed into dust with great might
And so one cold wet day, the unicorn and dragon went away
And there in that strange land they are living to this day.

Ten Flying Fishes

Michael Bate (9)

Ten flying fishes flying back in time
One passed away then there were nine.

Nine flying fishes opening the gate
One got locked out then there were eight.

Eight flying fishes going to Devon
One didn't know the way then there were seven.

Seven flying fishes picking up sticks
One got eaten by a fox then there were six.

Six flying fishes learning how to dive
One drowned then there were five.

Five flying fishes walking very low
One fell down a hole then there were four.

Four flying fishes bathing in the sea
One got eaten by a shark then there were three.

Three flying fishes trying on a shoe
One fell off his chair then there were two.

Two flying fishes going, going, gone
One disappeared then there was one.

One flying fish shone and shone
Burned and sizzled then there were none.

A Poem About Rowan

Jan Hiller

Rowan was an adventurous lad
to visit the moon
was his latest fad.

He purchased a very large balloon
and on a night in middle June
he took flight and very soon
was caught up in a freak typhoon
and buffeted in torrential rain
poor Rowan began to feel the strain.

A bumpy landing on a foreign shore
left him feeling very sore.
There he met a large baboon
brandishing a long harpoon
which by chance pierced t' balloon
leaving Rowan lost in gloom.

However on a bass bassoon
the friendly ape now played a tune,
too low in pitch for Rowan to croon.
By other means with words unspoken
the deadlock was quite quickly broken,
and very soon.

Rowan acting like a goon,
and baboon dressed as pantaloon
pranced a lively rigadoon
beneath the radiant silvery moon.
Suddenly the dream was broken,
far too soon - Rowan had woken.

Birthdays

Jane Byers

Come children to my house at one,
it's Lucy's party for just a day.
There're cakes and trifles, party hats too,
musical bumps if you care to stay.

Five I believe is a wonderful age of
innocence, loveliness and bliss,
please come to this before you have your first kiss!

Pipe Dreams

John F Murray

As he wafts his smoke, pipe dreams evoke.
That tobacco's one expensive joke.

Another match and another puff.
Then ask a friend for a pinch of snuff.

For that Sir Walter Raleigh, couldn't know the pleasures he would mix.
As besides his liking for good Queen Bess, there came bikes, and No.6.

And people flocked from all around, to try his new-found weed.
While taxmen rubbed their hands with joy, a duty, yes indeed.

So next time someone strikes a match, to light his cherished wood.
Be thankful spuds won't go in pipes, burnt chips don't smell so good.

The Daydreams Of Samuel

N Ferguson

Down near a mighty river,
Young Samuel sat one day
To watch the river traffic
And in dreams to drift away

He saw a mighty merchant ship
Outward bound for a far off land
Commanded by Captain Samuel
In a uniform so grand

Upon the bridge he'd strut and stride
Lieutenants standing by
He'd get this crew knocked into shape
Or know the reason why

Next he saw a gunboat
A naval man o' war
With bristling guns, torpedo tubes,
And pom-poms by the score

'Enemy aircraft sighted Sir!'
The lookout's cry came clear
'Stand by to engage!' Is the order given
And the crew began to cheer

'Mid smoke and grime,
That vision fades, as a little tugboat nears
Puffing and panting pompously
How important he appears

Down river he is heading fast
Must hurry, can't be late
'A giant liner needs my help
I dare not make her wait'

'He dare not make her wait, oh no!
Mum said be home by three!'
So homeward little Samuel turns
'I wonder what's for tea.'

All God's Children

Jocelyn Lander

Greetings to the Indian child,
Kin of Redskin warrior - wild.
Remember too the Eskimo
From far off lands of ice and snow.

We love brown-skinned boys and girls,
In their South Sea island worlds.
Not forgetting the Negroid race,
Love each piccaninny face.

We love Orientals, who -
Eastern ways of life ensue.
Then there are our Arab friends,
Kin of tribes with nomadic trends.

We love the West Indian child
From far Caribbean isle.
Look fondly on the Latin race,
Full of beauty, full of grace.

We'll always love our fair-skinned friends,
No matter what their creed impends.
World-wide, may they live in harmony,

Like one big happy family.

My Babysitter

Rebecca May Lister

While Mum and Dad were out last night,
A babysitter came round.
As soon as they left the house,
She'd fallen upon the ground.

I left my skateboard there for her,
I thought she'd like to see;
But with a scowl she hissed and said,
'You're trying to kill me!'

We played with sand and water next,
And I felt so much joy.
But she didn't see the funny side,
When I hit her with my toy.

I think I'll just be good for now,
She's looking rather tired.
Mummy's home, I'll look asleep
Or else she will be fired.

I like my babysitter now,
Next time I will be nice.
Instead of throwing mud at her,
I think I will throw rice.

The Wishing Tree

Eveline Hulme

I'd like a little wishing tree near the garden wall.
A tree with leaves as soft as silk and scented blossom, white as milk.
I'd like a little wishing tree that glowed on the darkest night,
And from my window I would see the fairies come to sing to me,
They'd nestle in the blossom on my lovely wishing tree.
I'd like to think at dead of night, if we wished hard enough,
That one wish would be granted before the early light.

Once Upon A Winter's Day

Irene Davison

Once upon a winter's day
a little snowman came along this way.
He started melting in the sun
and wasn't having too much fun.
I put him in the fridge for a while
that was better, it made him smile.
But every time I opened the door
he melted a little on the floor.
Mam came home and made my tea
and I am sure my iced-drink winked at me.

A Wee Bird's Tale

M McAteer

On Granda's window a birdie sat,
He was small and brown and wore a hat.
'Did you hear the news?' he said to me.
'What news?' I asked, as I made Granny's tea.
'It's all about your grandchild, Maeve,
She's the toast of the Baths, she's all the rave.'

'What did she do?' I asked, alarmed,
'Did she slip and fall? Was she badly harmed?'
The wee bird said, 'You're a silly blert,
Your grand-daughter has won a cert
For swimming ten long, tiring metres
And only swallowed fourteen litres.'

'You're telling lies!' I roared, 'you pup!
She can sink to the bottom but can't swim up.
I'll write to her da, the truth will come,
So flutter off or I'll kick your . . . er . . . leg.'

He started to go and raised his hat,
'I'll tell you more, old Granda Matt.
She wrote a note to her dad - home late,
Telling the story that couldn't wait;
And he was glad, and Sarah and Moll
And Mum - they all felt ten feet tall.
So that's the news, you'll find it's true.'
Then spreading his wings, away he flew.

Eyes Of A Child

Mary Robinson

A child gazed into shop window - looking at toys on display
That doll - oh that it were mine - to help make a happy day
For I could have a pretend - my friend - always to be
Since my best friend Polly - has gone away from me
We were always playing happily - now we are miles apart
Mummy does not understand - I have a lonely heart
Polly came into my life - parents - she had none
She was borrowed a short while - from a special home
I do so wish she was here now - to hug her oh so tight
This dolly could not be the same - to sleep with every night
Shiny star - bright in sky - can I wish on you?
I promise to keep silent - make it all come true
Can Polly stay with me for keeps - my lucky number three
We can play together - even climb a tree
The table looks so empty - when she's not sitting there
What is the word grown-ups say? - Oh yes - 'despair'
At home, the child is silent - very deep in thought
The door is slowly opened - 'Mummy have you bought
Another toy for me - can't I have my dearest friend?'
'Yes' said Mum 'we have all missed out - be it not the end
Your sweet Polly comes tomorrow - to stay for evermore.'
That child let out squeals of delight - like a lion's roar
What a happy moment - this special news could be
To make a lovely ending - for a complete family.

30 Lines For A Child

Mel Jordan

When you are 1 you'll start to walk
By the time you are 2 you'll know how to talk,
And when you are nearly 3 years old
You're mummy will tell you to do what you're told.

You'll be going to nursery in a little while
And what you do there will make you smile,
You can paint a picture or play with the toys
Along with all the other girls and boys.

On Christmas Eve Santa Claus will bring
All what you asked for and some other thing,
Go to bed early and go straight to sleep
And promise your mummy you won't even peep.

Now it's time for the infants' school
And you'll start to understand,
That you must always obey the golden rule
And never hold a stranger's hand.

After the infants, you're ready to move on
To the juniors and this is better,
The little school has been and gone
And now you can write Mummy a letter.

You'll be here 'til the age of 11
And you'll really enjoy the new stuff,
But don't ever believe it's like heaven
If you're given a ciggy to puff.

The first thing you do is say *'No'*
And then run away from the scene,
Then tell the teacher that you know
Of someone naughty and where they had been.

If you want to stay smart and no mug
You must always say *'No'* to the drug.

Teacher Was An Alien

Malcolm Ward

To all the other teachers, Miss Jones had seemed quite strange,
Perhaps it was the extra eye, or the way her colour changed
From red to blue with yellow spots, and her hair from pink to grey
Depending on the temperature at certain times throughout the day.

Or perhaps it was her curly tail, or her quite uncanny knack
Of writing on the blackboard with her hands behind her back.
But whatever, there was something that just didn't seem quite right
And the staff room rang with gossip whenever she was out of sight.

But the children never noticed, or they simply didn't care,
To them she was a teacher who was good and kind and fair.
Her lessons were enjoyable, they learned their ABCs,
And she taught them how to balance jammy doughnuts on their knees.

They learned their twelve times tables in five languages at least,
There was Russian, Dutch and German and a couple from the East.
And they still had time for nursery rhymes that they learned from
                                        front to back,
Like 'Winkie Willie Wee' or their favourite 'Jill and Jack'.

But science they excelled in, and though only six years old
They manufactured penicillin out of bits of smelly mould.
And they learned of astro-physics and of travelling through space,
Whilst Einstein and his theories put a smile upon their face.

They never did discover what happened to Miss Jones,
They never found a body or a pile of rotten bones.
She simply disappeared, though the children, so it's said,
Found the scorch marks of a rocket round behind the cycle shed!

A Day In The Life Of A Knight

Jeff Jones

Long ago, in days of old
Of tournaments when knights were bold
There was one whose name was never known
His face was covered by a mask
But he was up to the task
Of sword, lance and mace
But no one ever saw his face
His horse was strong and shiny black
And carried the knight upon his back
Complete with weapons and armour too
To fight and win the whole year through
At country fairs he would compete
Thrilling crowds with his feat
Of courage, skill and strength
Taking the trophy at some length
Then one day, in combat bound
Both horse and knight fell to the ground
A deadly hush throughout the crowd
The knight, rising with head bowed
He kneeled and stroked the jet-black hair
But it was clear there was no life there
He went away, is heart in pain
That knight was never seen again . . .

Katy Organ (15)

Sneezing, wheezing, coughing and choking

Rope, leather,
woolly jumper.

Mother dear smeared across my face
with spitty tissues.
We are a meaningless race,
chasing an ongoing dream.

Dying, lying. Wishing to be free.
Seeing nothing but
open
nothingness
wide.

Vast spaces

space.
Needing, wanting but not having
never having.

Children Of Poverty

Cheryl Louise Williams

A child sits quietly all alone
She wonders why she has no home.
No toys, no school, no teddy bear,
No somebody to really care.

Her mum and dad can't take the strain,
Nowhere to live, nothing to gain,
No helping hand to see them through,
No job, no money, what can they do?

There're hundreds like her and they all will be,
Millennium children of poverty,
Trapped where they are, no means of escape,
Somebody help them, what will it take?

The world is supposed to be a better place,
But life for them has a bitter taste,
A cruel test of fate maybe,
Can we change our destiny?

Why?

Rachel McAviney (13)

We plodded through endless marsh in this glorified hell,
As from the sky rained down shell after speeding shell.
Crippled from over-weighted sacks,
And like dominoes, man after man fell.

The cry of 'Gas!' A sound familiar now,
I strained for my mask as quickly as my aching fingers would allow.
An instant green world flashed to my vision,
And sweat continuously dripped from my furrowed brow.

There were some not so lucky, and though they did try,
They choked the unthinkable and had fear in their eye.
They had left it too late and knew of their fate,
But what was the cause for all these people to die? Why?

Six

J Bunnell

Speaking as a child, aged six,
I feel as if I'm in a fix,
my parents tell me what to do,
they think they know what's best for you.
Brush your hair,
clean your teeth,
make sure you brush underneath.
Eat your meals,
stand up straight,
run to school, don't be late,
don't climb trees, you may fall,
stop jumping off the garden wall.
You mustn't pull the doggy's tail,
don't hammer in Daddy's nails.
Go to sleep, it's getting late,
stop swinging on the garden gate.
Watch the cars,
mind the roads,
use your hanky,
don't pick your nose.
Please be quiet,
don't act daft,
stop drawing on the garden path.
But speaking as a child, aged six,
who was feeling in a fix,
when Mum and Dad kiss me goodnight,
I think that maybe they are right.

Alys's Lump

Amanda Brooks

She had a poorly gaze and a damp hot head,
'Keep an eye on Alys' the doctor had said.
But she gave her Mum and Daddy a terrible fright,
when her neck grew a lump in the middle of the night.

We went to the hospital to see Dr Owen.
'Come back,' he said 'if it keeps on growing.'
The weeks went by and the medicine did nothing,
Alys seemed quite happy but the lump kept growing.

Mummy and Daddy were getting very worried,
so back to the hospital with Alys they hurried.
Dr Cambell said 'It's time to do some tests,'
'so take off her clothes and take off her vest.'
She had blood tests, X-rays and CT scan,
The anaesthetist was a lovely man.

Then finally, one Monday, after an eight week wait,
Nain and Elin waved goodbye at the garden gate.
Alys went to hospital in the big silver car
to exchange her lump for a neat little scar.
Then the lump went away to be poked and checked,
to see why it caused such a problem in her neck.

Now Alys feels much better, she will never recall,
how her lump caused such worry and concern for us all.
A blue-eyed baby with blonde, shiny curls.
We are so proud of Alys,
She is a brave little girl.

Untitled

S Huntley

As I walk down the street
Claire and Debbie, my friends I meet.
With pure white snow upon the ground
A dream of Disneyland here I found.

On some rides, to and fro
Up and down, high and low
Faster and faster, round and round
Oh look there's Mickey on the ground

Candyfloss and chocolate, doughnuts and chips
let's loop-the-loop and down big dips
But what has happened? I'm back where I started!
So me and my dream, we are now parted.
Never again will I dream such a dream
So Disneyland will never be seen.

Eclipse '99

Lorna Gammage (13)

It's the 11th day of August,
In 1999
There's a total eclipse in Cornwall,
And everyone's praying that it will be fine.

Early on it seems quite promising;
The sky is very bright.
And all of the people
Are looking forward to the amazing sight.

As the historical event draws nearer,
Clouds cover the sky.
But this doesn't dampen anyone's spirits
As something begins to happen up high.

It's just past 9:55
And the phenomenon has begun.
It looks almost as if someone is hungry
And has taken a bite out of the sun.

An RAF Hercules is flying above the clouds
Recording everything
Sending pictures down to earth
TV viewers don't miss a thing

There's not long to go now;
Totality is approaching fast
For just under two minutes
Will this darkness last.

People are getting excited
As 11:11 draws near
The moon shadow sweeps across the sky
At last - it's finally here!

An eerie hush falls over everything
Not a sound can be heard
No noises from any cars or animals
Not even a 'tweet' from a bird

It's almost like having midnight at midday
Outside seems almost black
Someone sets off some fireworks
And then suddenly, daylight creeps back.

The incredible spectacle is over
But the memory will live on
In the minds of all those who witnessed it
When the moon passed in front of the sun.

I Wish I Was

Katie Reilly

Oh, I wish I was a Rainbow Guide
To have friends and leaders by my side,
I'd lend a hand and be kind to all,
I'd have great fun with a beanbag or ball.
I could paint pictures and take them home
To cover Mum's kitchen or the Millennium Dome!
I'd sing along to tunes, old and new
And take part in quizzes, dog jogs too.
I'd do some dancing and colouring in,
Find the donkey's tail with a silver pin.
Make masks and headbands and crafts galore
I'd be so good, I would want to make more.
I would make up a poem or even a prayer
Just to show others I really do care,
I would make a necklace, bracelet and rings
I would love my God and all those things.
I'd love to go to a meeting . . . it's just through that door
Maybe next year . . . as I am only four!

Mary The Fairy

Deborah Findlay (6)

I had a little fairy
Who had a little wand
Her name was Mary
And she lived beside a pond

She was very pretty
With silver wings
She had a fairy kitty
And lots of other things.

Animals

Carol Roberts (6)

Look at the little frog
Who sat on the log today
Croak, croak, croakety croak

Look at the little foal
Who ate the juiciest grass,
Neigh, neigh, neighety, neigh
So that's the fun for today.

My Little Rabbit

Alice Cheape (5)

I have a little rabbit
It is the colour of toffee
And the colour of tea
And the colour of coffee

She hops around the garden
And jumps among the flowers
Eats all the grass
So we don't need a mower

Knock, Knock

Ellise Alexander (7)

Knock, knock,
Who's there?
Open the door
If you dare!

Rainbow Guides

Kristi Brimer (6)

Rainbows are good
'Cos there's lots to do
We sing and we play
And we make things too

Rainbows are good
They do as they're told
They help other people
Young and old

Rainbows are good
It's on Thursday nights
And the week without it
Wouldn't seem right.

The Fairy

Abigail Rogers (6)

I had a little fairy in my garden
She was so pretty
She wore a crown of flowers
She had silver wings and a wand and things

And she had magical powers.

Harry

Rebecca Davis & Mrs Davis

I have a dog called Harry
He's really very mad
He digs big holes and chews my toys
He's really very bad
He runs away outside the house
And won't do as he's told
But he's soft and fun and very cute
I'll love him till he's old.

Gardens

Rachael Woodley (6)

Gardens have flowers
And trees
And buzzy bees,
Wasps' nests, holly bushes,
Birds that sing and nettles
That sting.

Lorna May And Me

Joan Tyler

I'm just about to read a book
I'll read it upside down
My best friend will read it too
We will never make a sound

Lorna May will read it backwards
She's extremely good at that
I think we will go to her house
And read the whole book rack!

I would just about give anything
For just one little look
But I only see the downside
Of someone else's book

We could visit the library
No television's there
It's quiet educational
We are an academic pair

My brother says Lorna May's pretend
Be quiet and watch the box
Mum says that if she's real
She would have writing on her socks!

Dad is on the Internet
And says just let her be
After he has finished he'll
Read to Lorna May and me.